Acknowledgements

Earlier versions of the following poems have appeared in the following journals:

"My Mother's Ink," in *Inkwell*; "Shinto Mama," in *Italian Americana*; "An Italian in Nature" and "Your Cousin Dominick," in *The Paterson Literary Review*; "Galdiator's Labyrinth," "*Italianità*" and "Jimi Hendrix Influences Italian American Parents from Brooklyn," in *Perspectives*; "Asking Directions" and "With three women, none a wife," in *Vivace*; "Fear of Crossing Over," "In Italian American T. V. Commercials," "*L'Intagliatore*," "*Napulitàn*" and "Poets are good at forgetting," in *Voices in Italian Americana*.

Also by George Guida

*The Peasant and the Pen:
Men, Enterprise and the Recovery of Culture
in Italian American Narrative*

Dedication

For my parents, Mary and George Guida,
for everyone else who's taught me the culture,
and for everyone curious about it.

Table of Contents

I'm through being Italian   1
Italianità   4
An Italian in Nature   6
Upon Discovering I Am Part Genovese   9
Capelli ancora bagnati   11
What Happens to a Man
on the East Side of Manhattan   12
Garibaldi's House   14
L'Intagliatore   15
Scacciatt', sciaquatt', sciangatt'   17
The Italian American Satan   19
Shinto Mama   20
THE BACK TO ITALY MOVEMENT   22
Napulitàn   28
The Sal and Joey   31
In Italian American T. V. Commercials   33
Tonight's Italians   35
Noi uomini   37
When We're Italian   38
With three women, none a wife   41
A Fine Piece of Yesteryear   42
Asking Directions   44
Fear of Crossing Over   46
Languizz'   47
The Academic Tarantella   48
Italian Suit   50
BASTARDO GRASSO   51
Italians, Beware   52
Over Cell Phones   53
The *Goscias*   55
The Last Italian American Poetry Reading   57
Soggiorno   59
Sinatra Drive   61
Tina Scandul   64
A Fondness for Absent Flowers   66

Gladiator's Labyrinth   67
When Your Favorite Poet Dies   68
Poets are good at forgetting,   69
Italian New Year   71
My Mother Moves to Vermont   73
My Mother's Ink   74
Traditions   75
Your Cousin Dominick   76
Jimi Hendrix Influences
Italian American Parents from Brooklyn   77
Barney on Long Island   78
Down These Very Nice Streets
or The Endless Conversation   80
Germocc' and *Gebucc'*   83
Alma Mater   85
Aeneas   86
Why Italians Will Save the World   88
I'll Never Die Italian   89
Ci sentiamo   90
La vita sarebbe bella anche se   92
Life would be fine even if   93
REPEAT AFTER ME   94
Personal References   96
Zen Italian   97
An Italian Friend   98

I'M THROUGH BEING ITALIAN

Long hours
Rotten pay
And where's the satisfaction?

I show up every morning
with my olive skin,
my Roman nose,
my deepset eyes,
my stubble,
my curls,
my squat body,
my smooth voice,
comic gestures,
tragic soul,
aria in my heart,
recitative on my lips,
stories always at the ready,

and set them down
the way I think Dante would
if he had survived translation,
but who sees them?
Who understands?

I'm through being Italian
because they won't let me back into Italy.

The town my forbears built
says I need a government *permesso*
to set foot in the little *piazza*
where dogs sleep
and the pensioned men
afraid I'll take a job they couldn't use
roll up their sleeves
to play checkers and drink *vino*
in the sun,
which gives their skin its healthy glow.

Low Italian

Countless Euros, *tanti soldi,*
so I can stay a season
and, if they'll talk to me,
learn the dialect,
request dried flowers
of a distant cousin's florist
to decorate my America.

I'm through being Italian,
because no one here knows the words.

Over the holidays
I ask the supermarket butcher,
Hey, buddy, can I get *cabuzell'* for twelve?
He looks at me as if
cabuzell' were a controlled substance.
You want a *what*? he thinks.
Ca-buzz-ell', I think back,
and a pound of *suffrit'*,
and while you're at it,
two nice bunches of *scarol'*.

No one in America will admit
these things exist,
so as a patriot
I try to tell them
they can live without
fast food and football.
Instead let's talk, I say.
Italians, the ones I know,
like to talk, expect to talk
while they eat, oh yes,
and drink sambucaed coffee
and tell stories that don't have to be true,
and argue without having a point.

But while I share that life,
try to live it,
theirs passes me by.
They make quiet money,

live in homes with views,
summer,
take up golf,
weary,
repeat the process elsewhere.
while I sit here
with my incongruous graces,
family,
and little else.

Italianità in America
is my Beatrice,
but no one thinks she's beautiful
I'm not so sure myself,
so I've been writing lines
of loves and hatreds
no one feels, no one understands
to a few who believe they might.

Now, my red and green pen
is almost empty,
and since no one can refill me,
I'm telling Beatrice, Go to hell,
telling myself for eternity
I'm through being Italian.

Low Italian

ITALIANITÀ

Selling it like the morning paper, 1897,
hawking it, telling
a hawk from a handsaw
for an audience of twenty-five
bona fide oppressed minorities
who ask how
I can speak with authority
of non-standard English.

Italglish is, I say, what my grandfather spoke,
never having met the man,
never having spoken it myself,
though in my writing, some say,
that's what I do.
We (meaning I) then, I say,
value blah blah blah all Englishes
blah blah blah deep structure
bee bee bee, boo boo boo, baa baa baa,
but all need an English to share with
imaginary Guamites and Sri Lankans
who would not understand Italglish,
thinking Black English, Spanglish, New Yorkese,
all the time I'm saying.

Italglish, circa 1897, could have lived
like the tangled roots of teeth adrift
in the mouths of darker, shorter, mustachioed,
mandolin-strumming, macaroni-devouring
bygone, foregone tillers of rocky soil.
who left Italian in the morning for work,
returned to it by twilight,
feeling it before they felt it,
like warm beds, cool sheets,
corrupted Latin words of love
whispered in wives' soft arms.

I am often mistaken for Jewish
by white folks; by others
I am often mistaken for white folks.
I pick my ethnic teeth for old food,
pick my ethnic guitar,
pick at my polenta
which arrives as an appetizer
to a meat course I buy dearly.

My name is "tiller of the soil,"
but I teach English grammar
dogging me down the hours to night,
like a clogged sinus, a Kansas summer,
self-loathing,
the English whispers of my Nordic lover.

Italglish!
Won't anyone buy my Italglish!
Genuine article!
Handed down from *Nonno, Nonna!*
Straight from the old country!
Like fine wine!
Italianità!
(maybe though 100 years old, undrinkable)

Low Italian

An Italian in Nature

I amble East End byways
where the old Italians settle,
to stare at swans, herons, loons,
the last bird a family label
for anyone not them,
not remotely Italian.

The nature poets annoy me,
their passion cropped,
comprehension of mind confined
to platitudes and deciduous plants.
They have no ideas, no idea
Italians take nature for granted,
for culture.

The old summer manses here
always lured nature poets.
I can tell by lawns rolling to dockage,
wisely placed pines.

Product of Italian gardeners,
this order appeals to my senses
shaped by Brooklyn's flower boxes,
long fellowship strolls
along Tuscan hill paths.

People don't think of Italians in nature,
though that's all we have,
human nature,
the art of self as center,
alone in the world,
alone in eternity,
linked to all humanity
by ruin and masterpiece.

All the world's humanity disappears,
as I approach the town dock.
Mother ducks and ducklings

navigate the empty bay.
All the Italians have docked their boats
until the fish return.
What's the use of water without life?
I've been taught to think.

Alone in nature, I wander
the twin forks of Long Island,
the coves and harbors,
in search of tall tales,
tall ships bound for 1600,
when pines crowded shores
like tribes of green Indians
gathered to receive whiteness.

Christopher Columbus never belonged
to Greenpeace. Nature was already safe.

Do Italians belong in American nature?
Look what they do to suburbs:
Italian developers with anglicized names,
American construction firms
Italianized for prestige
paint landscapes with no perspective.
I can smell the strip malls
in the distance, five-acre lots
posted for sale, commercial zoning.

But I am not a nature poet.
I am not a protest nature poet.
Nature, I believe, will come and go
as it pleases, like an Italian
told how to think.
This is the world's eternal culture.

Sacco and Vanzetti died labeled
anarchists. They mistakenly came
to believe in the power,
cruelty and potential
of anything other than a tree.

Low Italian

My favorite weeping willow
caresses planked membranes of Mud Creek.
My blue heron glides
between canopy and ripple,
toward western twilight orange.

Is this a picture?
The Italians of Renaissance history
would have settled here to paint it,
would have crafted easels of willow branch,
would have slept
not in the second bedrooms of post-War ranches,
like so many lost *nonni*,
but on canal banks lit by stars,
eyes ablaze, *à là Rafaello*,
souls ablaze at the world's touch.

George Guida

Upon Discovering I Am Part Genovese

I don't know what to think,
who lately have lectured on acts of larceny
against *contadini meridionali*
I thought were my sole begetters.

Now my red-haired, green-eyed *nonna*
turns out to be Genovese,
like pesto,
like the red-headed woodpecker
whose hammering troubles
my suburban Southern comfort.

Yesterday I was a victim.
Today I am beyond category, above class,
lost along a *via antica*,
between *città* and *latifondo*.
I am taking my identity day by day,
giornaliero, no, *signore*.

The bus from Avellino to *piccolo* Prata,
the *paese* of my people,
had me singing *"O sole mio!"*
weeping essential tears
that soaked the red shirt I had commissioned
for the trek to roots,
now the tears of a Northern snake.

Bastard child of miscegenation,
the thrill of my Nordic bride gone,
I am the diaspora's future,
when it is simpler to be its past.
How many dialects will I have to learn,
to speak the language of *antenati*.

But "Genovese" is just a word,
like Columbus, sound and fury,
like Garibaldi, just a red beard
that would have grown for any invading horde.

Low Italian

Through the valleys of Tuscany, Lazio,
I want to descend to Campania, Sicilia.
I want to forsake the lush Riviera
for *Mezzogiorno* dust,
to yell from the highest, driest peak,
"Liguria, let my ego go!"

I want to strike a crooked deal with myself,
detente with the North, and in return
the freedom of Southern *Miseria*,
memories of malaria,
daydreams of drought,
the call of *campanilismo*.

When I was Avellinese,
I lounged all day in the *piazza*,
now that the fields were overgrown,
now that the masses had fled
this cobblestone Italy of us
for the clatter and rumble of erstwhile them.

CAPELLI ANCORA BAGNATI

In Italy they waited
as I washed for *la cena*,
a half dozen *meridionali*, they waited
to yell, *"O,*
ecco il gran bastardo Americano
sempre con i capelli ancora bagnati,"
waited so we could walk in arms
through gray *Senese* alleys
—*"La vita è durissima"*—
through the lean streets of Siena,
through the purple and ocher Tuscan twilight.
to *la mensa*, vineyards in the distance
through cathedral windows and a sense
that time could do what it liked,
we would eat well, live
and die as we pleased.

In America I am never done
with *la doccia*. Bathroom window
breezes chill my shoulders,
suds warm my scalp,
clocks tick in my ears, friends
with hair blown dry
rush to empty tables.

The Italians taught me to say,
"La fonda è guasta" when the drain backed up
and pools of soothing water bathed my feet—
"The portal to the deep is spoiled"—
as I savored the unsolved problem.

Low Italian

What Happens to a Man on the East Side of Manhattan

He bears an Italian name. They tell him no.
The managing editor corrects his pronunciation
of virago (vee-RAH-go), a word of Italian descent.

He meets a woman, falls in love.
She tells him three things her man cannot be:
aspiring musician,
heavy drug user,
Italian.
She makes him an exception.

He takes a walk-up on 73rd,
views of brick and Hungarian refugees in beach chairs.
A business man named Whitney mugs him at the corner,
flattens him with a champagne magnum.

Mink stoles in heat call his name.
The echo buries him in an avalanche of snow queens.
The well-preserved in limousines
spatter slush on his jeans.

Neighbors whisper perfect English in his ear.
They forbid him to yell at the river.
They confine his urges to taverns.
They fill his head with veggie burgers.

No one will repair his disabled television.
He watches the radio.
He loses control of his laundry.

Cafès serve him Haydn and Mozart
in cups of weak espresso,
delis, less than that.
Chinese families send him questionably balanced meals.
Dogs walk their owners in his face.
The Bronx begins to stare him down through Hellgate.

Half-marathon runners dump his body
on a faux foam couch.
Antiques clog his living space.
Birds die of twittering at his window.
The mailman solders shut his box.
His faucet drowns his phone.
Footsteps slide videos under his door.
It snows.

An Italian saucier tells his blue eyes pesto is served
at room temperature.
Calabresi police keep track of his whereabouts.
A Neopolitan landlord rapes him from New Jersey.
He writes the state senate for justice.

Low Italian

Garibaldi's House

Not as grand as we had thought,
in the age of men small and grand.

His red shirt engulfed the sitting room.
We tried to climb inside the sleeves,
to hide ourselves in his fabric,
in the underbrush of his fiery beard.

Uno spiffero, in the drafty bedroom, you said
this is where he slept
and we wondered how
when New York Harbor held him hostages
to thoughts of a use for those grand hands
that now swept hallways
while Meucci whistled
Verdi's arias from the workshop.

What did he do as the morning sun
crept toward him from *Italia*?
He walked to the outhouse you showed us,
on the grounds near the old stone fence
separating the two Italians
from the nothingness of *L'America*.

We traced his steps.
We hoped to catch him before he disappeared
into a shack here
that lent him the comfort of desperation.

Back in the house
you showed us a documentary.
Garibaldi liked to sleep late on Sundays,
thinking *L'America* didn't need him.

Or else you would have left his memory
not a wooden house,
but something greater,
like a stone quarried from centuries,
placed in the garden for future use.

GEORGE GUIDA

L'Intagliatore

for Steve De Rosa

To the floor grey earth beneath his stool
flitter lambent flakes of Pear-
and Boxwood,
inhabit the ground around his easel,
dormant dust.
His hands alone mingle spirit.

His broad back sways, plane to plane,
right to left,
and slowly back.
Here and there
Aramaic glimpses of an inlaid halo, half,
a flushed Madonna's cheek,
and half an infant Christ,
half resting in a corner swaddled blue.

"There are twenty-eight angles in the child's face,"
he tells himself.
"At least I think,"
and so there are.

Cut fruits, juices captured,
Orange wedges and strips of peach,
sit on a plate of sacred heart relief.
He gropes for fruit
to squeeze with weighty teeth and syphon
juice from pulp,
to ignore a voice from the eternal kitchen,
to fuel the action of marvelous hands,
to resurrect the still life fruit
in three dimensions.
The child will be annointed
of transfigured fruit, orange, pear, peach, plum,
blessed of the Madonna's smooth and ancient hand.
He can banish her, if he chooses,

Low Italian

from his garden,
send her off to gaze at no one,
and wring the last clotted drop of hope
from a desiccated rind.

"Touch the wood,"
he tells his son,
a boy as tall as seated him.
"Run your finger over this...
feel it."
The furrows form a crown
ruby and gold, of the child,
the lines of thought
from his conscience to his idol,
worked to a high finish.
The boy is blind
and follows his touch.

An angel in the upper left,
innocent, sings circle-mouthed glee,
left wing half-formed,
furthest feathers submerged in wood,
feels the tug of oblivion,
and slips from the boy.

The woodcarver, manacled, sobs,
meekly extends the dubious end of his knife
to the boy, to the angel,
to himself.

GEORGE GUIDA

SCACCIATT', SCIAQUATT', SCIANGATT'

For years I have wondered how to spell these words
and what they mean.

Inside the pick-up's cab,
tiny flag of Italy dangling from the rear-view,
north from blue plate breakfast Pawtucket
to a Boston race track mini-*Mezzogiorno*,
Louis Prima busting from the tape deck,
I, a boy, rode with two dead horsemen,
briganti, cousin and uncle.

To them everything was
scacciatt', sciaquatt', or *sciangatt',*
scacciattella, sciaquattella, sciangattella,
a little shot, washed out, lame.
Their cheap cotton shirts perpetually *scacciatt'.*
the paint job on their rented house always *sciaquatt',*
their old horses forever *sciangatt'.*

No one translated.
Scacciatt' meant *scacciatt'.*
My cousin knew it from my uncle
who knew it from his father
who knew it from the wild *Provincia d'Avellin'.*
I knew what it meant.

I didn't know what it meant.
I grew jealous of *sciaquiatt',* of these words,
jealous that they poured like sweat
from blue collar landsmen
in the hot July cab
of two fat men and one fat boy
crammed together by hazy history.

My uncle and my cousin,
proud to be Brooklyn Italian
fled to New England
for sterner Americans, more desperate *paesans.*

Low Italian

Their days one long meal,
one practical joke, one rubber rat
on the owner's overcoat,

filling washed out American days
with Neopolitan song and sport
shoplifting shoes in the name of common justice
to the tune of "Santa Lucia."

Years later my cousin too young lay crammed in a coffin
two sizes too small, mourners by the hundreds,
his body *scacciatt', sciaquatt'* from outlaw life,
my old uncle *sciangatt'* in a hospital bed,
his final view of Boston Harbor.
This vocabulary of Fates defined
by simple minds and lives.

Now I try to spell these words,
but am too late to understand,
to have them on my tongue
like the taste of someone else's tears.

GEORGE GUIDA

THE ITALIAN AMERICAN SATAN

Thirty-three years old,
I refuse to father my parents' *nipoti*.

Once, at a Christmas family dinner,
I renounced my interest in Italian women.
Not my type, I declared,
turning from the table.

Intelligent, suburban, well-fed,
I have pursued
neither business, nor law, nor medicine.

One lazy Sunday morning,
I took a mailed photograph
of my second cousin's newborn
and threw it in the trash.

On the eve of my year in Italy,
I dressed up as the Pope
and had sex with my Jewish girlfriend.

Locked in my rootless room,
I spill my family's guts on paper,
overwhelming *omertà*.

And for this, other demons praise me.

Low Italian

Shinto Mama

She converted after 5:30 mass,
while watching The History Channel.

She had the gilt-framed family photos
down from the paneled wall.

"Wipe your feet, and keep quiet," she said.
"I'm worshipping Great Aunt Tessie."

"Aunt Tessie, Aunt Tessie!
Give the little *sfacim'* my daughter some common sense."

My mother hovers at an altar
to sere images of housecoated women
frowning, upon the brick stoops of Brooklyn.

She chants staccato,
"Ohm, ohm, ohm-ohm-ohm,"
semi-automatic.

My poor sisters in miniature,
made of excess tinsel and *presepio* figurines,
sit in her hands.

Her kimono the size of Sicily,
my mother has gone
Japanese, converse *Madama Butterfly*.

The narrator has told her
a Shinto priestess can summon spirits
of ancestors bound to serve their own.

She understands this guilt by blood.

"Uncle Martin, Uncle Martin!
Let my cheapskate brother, that *murte fam,*
pick up a check now and then.

What do I look like,
a friggin' Brinks truck?"

Her prayers rouse suburbs from slumber.

Italian women with direct lines
to their *stramort'* are legion.
They conjure the dead,
whenever we don't behave.

Their pleas still the streets,
resound to us in dreams,
they already our gods.

Low Italian

The Back to Italy Movement

Marcus Garvey liked the idea,
the former slaves and their descendants
returning to the motherland.

So I thought
since we too,
descendants of former slaves,
find ourselves uncomfortable,
too comfortable in America
among the fallen masters,
we too should consider
a movement
out of Boston, Chicago, and New York,
back to the *bel paese*.

I consider the possibility
of my mother borne on a white donkey
up the mountain road
to our ancestral *campano* village,
Prata del Principato Ultra,
a cluster of shacks and letters
she couldn't begin to decipher,
of her yelling, "How youse doin'?"
in Brooklynese, to unemployed men
playing *briscola* in the desolate piazza,
of official "Back to Italy"
repatriation guides
laying roses at my mother's feet
along the way
to the whitewashed stucco *chiesa*,
of old women, who could be great-aunts,
lining the processional route, all frowns,
of my mother searching for a shop,
a face that bears a family name,
and then
I consider the possibility
of everyone in the village being my cousin.

George Guida

Like Jefferson,
I consider the commonweal,
twenty million of us
calling Alitalia for last-minute reservations,
all'italiana,
gathering ourselves with difficulty,
negotiating
with our Irish and Jewish
halves and spouses,
returning en masse
to the massifs of Calabria, to the Abruzzi,
to Campania, Apulia, Molise, Lazio,
Sicilia, of course, and even Le Marche.

We would take along our names
(Many of them Germanic,
though to Germans
an Italian Americans Back to Germany Movement
might seem the end of history.).
We would take our names
and ply them like trades,
seeking out offices and kitchens
of *le famiglie*.

I consider
that more of us speak Spanish than Italian,
and all we know in dialect
is how to swear.
I see my father
arriving at Leonardo da Vinci Airport,
greeted by a great-uncle
to whom his first words,
also in Brooklynese, are
"*Buon giorno. A fissa e sorata!*"
I see my Italian-less mother
confused by a clerk, yelling to me
across a supermarket,
"What the hell is an *etto*?"
or asking an unsuspecting bartender,
in English, if he knows where she can find

Low Italian

a place she thinks they call a *cicicceria*
or maybe it's a *gacceria*,
like a *pizzeria*, but different,
a place that might serve *sfugliadells*,
pastry for which she has *ooli*.

I consider what will happen
when we all go back to Italy
with our *Ameriganishkeit*
and demand lawns and public golf courses,
malls, megastores, and multiplexes,
and what we get instead
are *vicoli* and bocce courts,
piazze, piccoli negozi, and dubbed *cinema.*
Half of us, like our distant kin,
will turn communist,
the other half, well...

I consider our Americanness,
wonder if Italians could teach us
to care again for voting,
train us to drink bottled water
at room temperature,
convince us that
"legal" and "normal"
are rarely synonyms,
driving is an art,
lying is a game,
love, a sport,
soccer, a true religion,
clergy were meant to be mocked,
and real fun is doing nothing.

But I can't crush our movement
before it begins,
so I consider the upside.
This is, after all, Italy we'll be going back to,
not Siberia, not Greenland,
not Rome, New York.

George Guida

I consider my parents again,
resettled in,
telling me they're off to the local *duomo*
(which they pronounce "domo")
to meet in its shadow new Italian friends,
to exchange nods,
and with the help of an interpreter,
recipes for *aglio-oglio*.
They will dine with Brunelleschi's scions
in the finest *osterie*,
yet claim still
they can get better bread in Brooklyn.

Most of us will like the food.
We may not understand the pizza,
but we'll compensate
by reacquiring the taste for *alic'*,
anchovies strewn over vermicelli
our neighbors will offer us
in trade for pot roast.

We will all learn the story of Garibaldi,
in the process forget some of Lincoln.
We will learn more truth of Mussolini
from EUR and bigotry
than from blackshirt uncles.
We will learn who Totò was.
We will learn to drink espresso standing up.
We will learn to spend a night discussing.
We will learn once more to live
among others.

I consider us waking up
in our natural habitat,
in an apartment
on the sun-dappled Piazza Navonna
or a *casina* in sun-drenched Salerno
or even a garrote in Spacca-Napoli,
crusing the Costiera Amalfitana,
top down, a thousand feet up,
Beach Boys on the radio

Low Italian

until we adjust to Pino Daniele,
and once we do, stopping
to walk naked along the rocky shore,
driving down to Sicilia
to affirm our blackness,
then back through heartland Italia,
to contemplate Assisi,
our place in the Italian cosmos,
on to Alba
for *carne cruda* and a glass of barbaresco,
a nip of *grappa*,
across the boot
to the marshy suburb of Malcontenta,
across the Venetian Lagoon
to the flickering Torcello
where we will set up something,
like Colonial Williamsburg,
preserve the vestiges
of our early American interlude:
social clubs, wedding shops,
red velour couches, guinea t-shirts:
a living museum for native tourists.

And I consider
that wherever we go, the people
will tell us wonderful stories
of the people whose *paese* we just left.
Like America, all this,
only unconsciously beautiful.

Finally, I consider the logistics.
Getting it all together will be like
inviting twenty million relatives
to Christmas Eve Dinner
without anyone complaining
there's never enough
fried *calamad'* to go around,
and didn't anyone remember
to make the *pulpo*?

Maybe we can resurrect Mr. Italy
for his final ad: reaching out
across the airwaves to the IA nation,
summoning us to the Jersey Shore,
a four-mile stretch to be announced,
our point of embarkation.

But if you reject this plan,
I'll have to fall back on the old ways,
and get it started *così*:
I'll call my aunt in Brooklyn
and find out who she knows.

Low Italian

NAPULITÀN'

I woke up today feeling
a little *Napulitàn'*
   a little like crying
   a little like singing
   a little like throwing
      a little extra cheese on my pizza
   a little shorter
   a little darker
   a little dreamier than usual
Napulitàn.

I woke up today
and sucked the life from a raw egg
wandered to work
where my eyes met yours
   and even though I knew without asking you
   asked
   "*Napulitàn'?*"
      "No," you replied
      "today I feel a little *Barese*
      a little like talking
      a little like working
      a little like a Greek
      a little like throwing
      a little extra cheese on my orecchiette
      a little lighter than you
      a little more sober
      a little more serious than usual
      you know
   Barese."

I nodded, understanding completely
continuing not to work
   when along came the boss
   who cursed me up and down
   for losing the company's mail
      for wasting the company's time

for being a little too *Napulitàn'*
he said
to which I paid no attention
since I could see that *he* was feeling
    a little *Toscano*, a little *Veneziano*
    even a little *Milanese*.

Of course I should have said nothing
but feeling suddenly a little *Calabrese*
I turned to him and said
    "*Va' fa' napula!*"
going on with my idleness.

Later that same day
I was staring across the pizzeria
at this fat slob
who looked *Pugliese* in the face
and *Tedesco* in the gut.
I was staring at the five slices on his table
when he caught me.
    "What's the problem, Pal?" he yelled
    "you feelin' a little *Laziale* today
    or what?"
Having already crossed the line
I looked him right in the eye
and said low, like a killer
stabbing each syllable with my tongue
    "No way, Fat Boy. *Na-pul-i-tàn'*
    not too hungry
    not too thirsty
    not too thin
    not too fat
    Napulitàn'
    but the way you're wolfing down those five slices
    I can tell you must be feeling yourself
    more than a little *Bolognese.*"

No sooner did the *-gnese* leave my lips
than his face turned absolutely *Siciliano*
He threw over his table and charged.
I let him come and then very *Piemontese*

Low Italian

stepped aside at the last second
letting him run head first
through the plate glass window
onto the sidewalk, like *un Sardo*.

By this time I was feeling
pretty good about myself
    no longer completely *Napulitàn'*
    but pretty good
    in fact, I thought
    a little *Abruzzese*
    a little clever
    a little stubborn
    a little like not throwing
        a little extra cheese on my *pane duro*
    a little intellectual
    a little baronial even
so I went back to the office
and decided
even though I thought I knew the answer
to present myself to the *paesana* receptionist
bow a couple of times
and ask her opinion through my smile.
    "*Abruzzese?*" I asked
to which, looking me up and down, she replied
    "You still look like a guinea to me."

George Guida

The Sal and Joey

Oh, they really beat the Sal and Joey out of him,
and you could see after that
he was never completely Christopher.
After they kicked him in the Uncle Frank,
he started acting like a real Maria.

I said to your father,
get over there and grab that little Vinny
by his Pier Paolo.
But you could see he was a Carmine,
so we let him Paulie his way home.

Everybody today thinks he's a Vito,
when he's usually nothing
but a Dominick, an Angelo, a Bobby.

Every once in a while you meet a Gerard,
but then he's with some Camille
who you want to tell what she can do
with her Big Aunt Flo.

Ah, don't try to Anthony me.
You have one little Peppino,
and I'm supposed to get all Aunt Tessie over it?
And don't make out like you're the Pete
and I'm the Mario.

No, I don't know
what kind of Carmella got to your cousin,
that he went Crazy Sebastian.
He used to have a reputation as an Ercole,
but now certain people think
he might be a Fabio.

If you ask me, what he needs is
some Rocco in his Sonny.
And that piece of Antoinette he's with,

Low Italian

she could use a good shot
of Annabella in the Little Millie.

That's all the Theresa and Jen I heard this week.
Any more Carlo or Jimmy,
you give me a call.
Otherwise, take care of your Nino,
you freakin' Uncle Ralph, you.

George Guida

In Italian American T. V. Commercials...

...A husband yells to his wife,
   "*Porca Miseria*,
   Marie, you made this coffee *alla brucciat'*.
   Jesus, Mary and Joseph,
   now I gotta go to work all *scacciat'*."
His wife retorts,
   "*Fata 'n cul!*
   Let your *goomad* make your friggin' coffee for you,
   or
   go make a cup of Folger's instant.
   Just leave me in peace.

...A camera pans the length of a macaroni bar:
gnocchi con quattro formaggi,
penne all'arrabiata,
linguine alle vongole
steaming,
to be eaten.
A man appears,
white tuxedo, black bowtie.
He stares into the camera eye.
   "Are you ready to eat like a *gavonn'*?
   I mean like a real *murte fam'*.
   Then whaddya waitin' for?
   Don't be like the *Amerigan'*.
   Come down to the new
   Caputo's Macaroni Bar.
   It would be a sin for me
   to waste all this food."

...Two mothers compare their thirty year old sons'
dirty shirts in split screen.
Mother Number One says,
   "*Madonn*, what a mess my son made.
   This shirt's all *schifuz'*,

Low Italian

    grease everywhere from the car,
    sauce.
    What does he think I am?"
Mother Number Two commiserates,
    "My little *Ciccibell'*, the same way,
    always with lipstick on his collar
    from that *mignotta Irisce* girlfriend of his.
    And he has the *faccia dost'* to throw his dirty shirts
    in my hamper.
    Strunz 'e med'.
    At least he has the brain's God gave him
    to buy me a nice bottle
    of Super Formula Whisk.
She sneers at Mother Number One.
    "He loves his mother."

...A young couple sits talking to a bank officer.
    "You know, Mr. Ladrone, we threw all our money
    into stocks,
    and then the market went south,
    and now we don't have *gaboicchia*.
    What are we gonna do?"
Ladrone rubs his chin.
    "What are you gonna do?
    Let me tell you something,
    Mr. and Mrs. Scacciasoldi.
    Don't listen to these *stunada* bastards
    on CNN.
    Put your money where your balls are
    with Marea mutual funds.
    With Marea you always know what's what.
    And besides, this is America,
    the greatest country in the world.
    What are you worryin' about?"

George Guida

Tonight's Italians

I don't want to write poems with dramatic tension,
as my Italian editor says I should.
Drama is for television.

He is not one of tonight's Italians.

Here we are,
a lovely Bolognese and quantity of Chianti
flushing our systems.

Here in Middletown, Connecticut
we are Italians: two Brooklyns, one Roma.

Dinner takes three hours,
with wine and courses
and colleagues and essays
and languages and contrasts
of cultures and women and sauces.

Two Brooklyns, one Roma,
three Italians repair to the t.v. room.

We tune to a program made art
by *Times* columnists in full parade of ignorance.
Our village elder debates
benign racism with his own hackles,
though we all three are here.
We volley make-believe mafiosi
like hard *palle* over brittle nets.
Not many viewers know
how Italians adore volleyball.
Our eyes follow character arcs
in their fourth season of drama.

Here we are with a marble bust of Dante,
from the speakers whispers of Vivaldi
volumes of Italian history all around,
original photos of Senese alleys,

Low Italian

Sicilian seascapes,
lacrimae cristi on ice
and cool night air.

We must be with television now,
knowing every word of the drama to come,
the cultural significance
the familiar vulgarity,
the faded guilty pleasure,
like ancient fellatio,
the dialect words *scafuzz'* and *scustumat'*,

Withered by dinner and hours of musing,
we give ourselves over,
because this and we are Italian.

In a town where it is easy
to lose oneself in oak groves,
wander lost through limestone lecture halls
named Hamilton, Washington, Stevens, Faulk,
we have gathered to sing ourselves.

Credits rolling,
we finish our maple ice cream cones.
Signor Roma travels home
through dark Connecticut.
We two Brooklyns would move then
to simulate stoop or *piazza* in the yard,
but, unused to so much company,
throats achy from wine and talk,
we stumble and slur our speech.

Noi Uomini

    We embrace in broad daylight,
        blow *baci*,
        hold hands and rub shoulders.

    We stare into each other's eyes,
        speak of romance, of lust,
            in low Italian.

      All of us paint on the side.
      We admire birds, flowers.
      We sip *espressi, cappuccini*, in gay caps.
    All of us can cook.
He is the maestro of *manicott'*,
        and I am the barone of *braciol'*.

Among women we never keep quiet.
    Among children we mother and father.
    Moments, stories break us down.
We wilt in the sun, pansies, you might say,

but

    while you call us names, remember,
    we know who you are.
      We slip, silken shadows, in and out
      of your homes, your women,
            carry them off.

    Remember,
    siamo noi
the men of Italian words.
    We are among you.
    State attenti,
if you know what that means.

Low Italian

When We're Italian

I knew I was Italian
when the phone rang,
      Brring-Ba-Da-Brring,
and I spoke, "Yeah, Hello?"
but like Marcello
      Mastroianni thought, *"Pronto, mi dica,"*
cavalier for a wide-hipped beauty
whose voice turned out to be my mother's.

I knew it
when my room looked *sciabliun'*
like a post-war Castellina-in-Chianti,
bottles of red rolled under beds,
dust afloat on fumes of *arucalirapp'*,
    the ruins of a modern Golden Age
      that lasted twenty minutes.

I knew you were Italian
when you met me,
called me *chiachieron'*,
    because I cracked jokes
while you, *dentista esperta, suora superiore*
numbed me, as that fine tool, your tongue,
extracted the past of my sins.

I knew it
when you called me pet names:
    Testa di Cazzo, Sporcacione
    Strunz', Maiale
    Ciucc', Cidrul', Caccasott'
    Porco Bastardo
and you smiled at my requital:
    Puttana minchiatta
    cagna, troia
    mignotta, bastarda
    brutta ragazacc'

before we made love to the strains
of "That Sonofabitch Colombo,"
smoked a cigarette
made like Garibaldis.

I knew we were Italian
when we argued meatballs,
        bread or no bread,
          one meat or three,
like Raffaello, Michelangelo
their dispute of hues,
as though they and not we were facing
        a living room to decorate,
            this *baracca* couch, *dove va? Ma no!*
                Come si fa?

We are always arranging
        not to look like gypsies
        or our neighbors.

I knew it
when we hewed a Christmas log
        for the child Christ,
and like *baroni* couldn't tolerate
            livestock on the lawn,
   so splurged instead,
bought Mary on the halfshell
        for *un po' di colore,*
        to make it nice,
        a little less *sciangatt'*.

I knew I was Italian
when like Ceasar I surveyed you
over a plate of pappardelle,
decided to cross the Rubicon
of your ruby lips,
        to reach simplicity itself
in phrases we both as children heard:
      "You'll see when you get older,
      the apple never falls too far."

Low Italian

In the end, you know, *tutto il mondo un paese*.
You conquer what you know.

George Guida

With Three Women, None a Wife

I have been to Italy
>paradise of lovers
>home of the Eternal

to learn the old ways
of family and friends

capture memories
to last a lifetime
>on film

turn to Capri, turn to the sea
and sigh and kiss and sigh
and say
>thank you for coming.

With three women, none a wife

>I have scaled the marble *scale*
>of Saint Peter's
>>praying for our future

>seeking out the Pope
>to ask his blessing
>out of wedlock
>>under the bleeding crucifix.

With three women, only one *metà italiana*

>I have verified on terraced hills
>*Italianità*
>as one or the other
>>staring at sunset

>conjured home
>bed
>French pastry
>>or the order of New York.

Low Italian

A Fine Piece of Yesteryear

Yesteryear crawls between the sheets.
We pursue *amore*

in the spirit
of *Settecento* don and courtesan,
a widow of *concezione*.
Her black shawl,
his dark sheets.
He barks our names.

I bark your name.
"*Malafemmina,*"
a modern canzone echoes centuries,
"*Femmina!*
Sei tu la più bella femmina!"
to a saucy disco beat.

We disappear into maroon 1970's
like Aldo Moro, another don
with his courtesan, laid low
by moral *assassini*.
Aldo Moro or another '70s Aldo,
the Bolla Soave man
who knew what women liked.

You are the only one ever to dig
centuries-old nails
into this Italic flesh.
Why must I connect the dots
that bounce from *Mezzogiorno*
to American Midnight?

Why must you know whence they came,
where they might go?

Andiamo!
We powder our faces and lower our bloomers

for the *pastore* of Majella
to toss into the sea.

They will drift
on eternal tides
until currents settle them
one at a time
on our naked backs, our thoughts,
molding all to a peasant sense of thighs.
Did I say thighs? I meant sighs.
Ah, but that's love.
History and I pursue *amore*.

Low Italian

Asking Directions

> "When asking directions in Italy, an inquiry to one individual very soon erupts into a group effort, with everyone within earshot joining in to offer an opinion."
> —Louis Inturrisi

> "You can...derive the vigor and vitality, the figurative quality, of your style, from the slang and racy expression of your lowly friends."
> —Hutchins Hapgood

I am a writer. I am Italian American.
    Italian hyphen American
    American hyphen Italian
    American slash Italian
    Italian backslash American
    American writer
    Italian writer
    Italian American writer

        I am, in other words, confused.
I am asking directions of people
    who have never traveled this road.
I am trying to follow the signs.
    I am lost.
    I am certain
        someone can tell me what I am.
        Opinions abound.
I am

"ethnic"
"mainstream"
"white"   "non-white"
    "straight"   "faggot"
    "male"   "romantic"
"self-indulgent"   "humorist"
    "contemporary"   "traditional"

"New York"   "academic"
"avant-garde"   "macaronic"
          "performance-oriented"
"poorly published"
                  "simply lacking"

How am I supposed to make sense
this foreign country's map?

Low Italian

Fear of Crossing Over

I too much fear speaking Italian,
that while trilling an r
my tongue will get stuck
and stay that way.

I too much fear eating Italian,
that I'll continue to like it too much.

I too much fear fighting Italian,
that I'll either give up and go home
or pull out a baseball bat and go to jail.

I too much fear loving Italian,
the damage I'll do when I love and lose.

I too much fear carousing Italian,
that the wine will run out,
that the sex will turn out to be merely human.

I too much fear pledging Italian,
that I'll have to cheer soccer teams
and vote in every election
or never vote at all
and damn other dark races.

But most of all I fear
denying Italian,
unlearning it,
and leaving it to ghosts
who whistle tarantellas in my ear.

LANGUIZZ'

    the idea that
             history is repeating on you
             like a bad bowl of *zuppa di* mussels,
             of linguine,

as your old man said a thousand times,
             with the clams

    the suggestion that
             you have tasted this *brodo* before,
             ladled from the old world
                potbottom

    the notion that
             you can sample the *zabaglione*
             they whipped up in Caserta
             in 1910,

and will pay for later with decades of *agita*
             and *languizz*

    the riddle that
             begs you to know
             the burning in your chest
             from the burning in your throat

    the recollection that
             all our American triumph and tragedy
                is *agita*,

             while *languizz* is only that
                    which we can spew

Low Italian

The Academic Tarantella

You dance, you dance around the past
like it was shoved inside your pants.
You can't ignore it or get past it,
so you try to make it last.

In your quest for publication
you take an hour and a quarter
to explain Italian life
as an endless day of barter.

You grew up
speaking some Italian curses.
Now you try
and turn them into verses.

Your grandma made
salsicc' and ravioli
She had a dream your grandpa
was in league with Mussolini.

(Or so you say.
Or so you say.)

You sing, you sing, you sing the praises
of Italian Americana.
You're not so sure why it's so great,
but it really doesn't matter.

Every culture has its hooks,
and yours has music, crime, and food,
you praise or damn them as you please,
all depending on your mood.

You now live
in suburban luxury,
take a guided tour
through the streets of *Napoli*.

This makes you
qualified to say
Italians like to live their lives
as characters in a play.

(Or so you write.
Or so you write.)

Low Italian

Italian Suit

```
                You don't need
                      me
                  to tell you
                      who
                      you
                      are
                  politicians         years
One          local                well spent
Five       service of                       reliving the
Ten     in the       custom      when   money    gran
                                                brigantaggio
Twenty years       suggests you                    of
Thirty              let      buy       leather    Apulia
              Dark        your         loafers
                          blue                  Molise
                      clothes          Sicilia
                   do the talking           Calabria
                         to             Campania
                        your
                    motherfather
                      girl     son    to
                   painting   me     have
                      Italian   easy mornings
                     of                a job
                   nice love        strangled  with
                      your           good pay
                shoelaces binding
                to mama's girl
                                     and papa's job
                He wanted you        She wanted you to
```

GEORGE GUIDA

BASTARDO GRASSO

Oh, God,
don't let him be Italian!
But when I look again I know he is:
Una Faccia, Una Raza
The high school band is playing
pomp and circumstance.
He wipes his hands on
the untamed flare of his Hawaiian shirt,
smiles smiles of satisfaction,
as the sea of brown, tan and pink
faces under mortarboards
confirms his suspicions
to cousins who have gathered
in G.I. haircuts and GAP funereal,
to watch his daughter march
into the future,
which means he has progeny.
His smirking stomach distended
for all the wrong reasons
points to the student choir,
who sing the gospel
in soulful tones
that spring from the scrutiny
of gutless guts like his,
as he whispers without thinking
that pretty soon in this district
they'll all be black.
He is all that people think we are times four,
a math that cancels the positive sum
of my graduate sister's equation to her friends,
and equals phone calls to his buddies on the force,
who that night at our party firehouse will order me
to keep "your people" off the streets,
without explaining to me who my people are.

Low Italian

Italians, Beware

Russians are now our friends.
They're tailing us down festooned streets,
following us to Bensonhurst and Belmont:
on Arthur Ave, Kosova's Florist
on 86th Street, Russian-language ATM's.

They're on our tail because they like us
for what we are: not black or dark brown.
They've noticed whom we keep out.
They've noticed our occasional green eyes.
They've identified with our melancholy.
They've developed a taste for riceballs.
They wouldn't mind marrying in.

They think perhaps we'll stand together
outside *salumerie* and tea rooms,
defending traditional boulevards
with sleeves rolled up and bats cocked,
instructing our women to say
       in copied broken American,
"You can not talk wiz me
       because you are the black."
They think that we, so different from American,
will want to join with them, a new race apart,
will want to stand with them, when
I see in silent corner dialogue now
Russian bear, Italian bull
smoking, surveying, glaring
and I wonder if we will.

Over Cell Phones

Call me ignorant, but I wonder,
can the Chinese understand each other
over cell phones?
Do their higher tones, like Yi and Mei
dissolve in sun spots?

The Chinese students in my class
do not sing the music of Cathay
as I teach them my Italian English.
Their mouths do not open
to answer me,
"Yes, we keep our cell phones off,
as you instructed."

The New York Chinese buy cell phones wholesale
from a factory in Shanghai Province.
They store them in a warehouse in Flushing, Queens.
This way they never beep or buzz or twitter,
create chaos from the order
of a class or walk or family meal.

Is it possible to stereotype a group
more than they do themselves?
Italian me, I wonder why *compare*
flash their phones like dago knives
at Brooklyn's throat,
complaining the Chinese (Koreans)
are taking over.

The Chinese have mastered cell phones
as tools of last resort, not instruments of pleasure.
They entomb them in plastic cases slipped in pockets,
not attached by clips to belts or waistbands,
turn them on only when the time is right,
when the tone of the message ceases to matter.

Low Italian

Yes, they understand each other.
They understand the beauty of their tongue
will not survive the flight from phone to phone.
Their tones recede in monosyllables
translated by satellite whim.

Can Americans and Italians
understand each other over cell phones
as they walk through Dyker Heights
or stroll down Via Banchi di Sotto?
Half the Italian language evaporates in unseen gesture,
while American English jams transmission.
All goes uninflected in this global conversation,
I think, as I jealously eye
the small black box
that Garrick Yue has,
or so he believes,
in secret pulled from his checkered coat,
singing monotone in a Chinese
that might as well be Italian.

The Goscias

"Did you see them?"
my mother asks my wife
each time we see
the little family-bred niece.

Italian thighs,
these *goscias* are your *goscias* too,
my mother wants to say,
though this is not our baby.

"Couldn't you eat them up?"
my mother wants to know,
though my wife is no cannibal,
and already gets the Italian drift.

"My little *cicc'*, she's a terror,"
for which my mother has spent
twenty years waiting,
for little kicks in the womb,
little kicks to cut expectant air.

"She's a chunk,"
with a bowl of pastina on her high chair.
"She's a *sfacim'*,"
with the bowl on the floor.

"She's a *mamdell'*,"
when she frowns
and tries to clean
the mess, my family,
in love with its only child,
has made.

"She's all the mother,"
claims my mother.
She too will grow up
to be her mother,
her face a cuneiform
of genealogy.

Low Italian

"I see the father too,"
because she flashes
an Italian grandmother's
idea of blackness
in an easy smile,
wiggles her behind, does
what our family left behind
in Naples, and denied
had ever arrived
from Africa.

"The *goscias*,"
my mother insists,
for they are hope
that my blond wife
will bear mainstream
American thighs
to walk the final new world mile.

"Did you see the *goscias*?
Could you eat them up?"
Could we really devour
this plump little shibboleth,
who babbles our bastardy
to a world of half-deaf ears,
to replace her with
an image of this world
that passed from us
before it was ever born?

George Guida

The Last Italian American Poetry Reading

The suggested donation at the door was
five thousand dollars.
An audience of coffee-colored, kinky-haired blonds
followed like children the circus spectacle
of two swarthy men with New York accents
grumbling, waving arms, adjusting the mic stand.

Inhabitants of a one-block stretch of Brooklyn
known as *Italoamericana Perduta*
herded the readers on stage.

Seven in all, eyes wild, stealing fearful glances
at the unfathomable, seated sea of assimilation,
they crossed to their marks
before the counter of a suburban McDonald's.

"I remember my grandmother," the first poet began.
The others scanned notebooks
for just the right regret,
since they all still loved the order of tradition.

Another, less certain of himself, declared,
"My love blooms like the tulips of Naples."

Another read a Petrarchan sonnet
about The Age of Macaroni,
the time before Americans ate pasta.

Another, an elegy for *Italianitá*,
on the outmarriage of her last remaining child,
and the confusion of a quarter Chinese grandson.

During the Q and A,
someone in the back row asked,
"Are you really all Italian?"
And one by one,
the poets named their dead,
explained away lacunae in the gene pool.

Low Italian

All questions answered,
the matriarch announced
they all would soon depart
for an island off Cozymel,
to people it with a race of new Italians
or extinguish their hot blood in the sea.

GEORGE GUIDA

SOGGIORNO

The double-decker five-ten Speonk train.

        I board the lower deck,
        steerage for Brooklyn Italians
        who thought big yards
        would change our lives.

        Clots of powdered sugar
        from my cappuccino muffin
        explode between my fingers.
        Saccharine whiteness streaks
        my black shirt.

        I am back at my mother's table,
        making a *gavonn'* of myself,
        now in public.

        The pig next to me writes
        his diary of a madman in beer.
        Fresh from a on-board *pisciat'*,
        he pulls *T.V. Guide*
        from his back pocket,
        and reads it like a novel.

At seven-o-two the train makes Mastic.

        I wait alone
        for the doors to open.
        Visible in the commuter lot,
        two Indian immigrants
        in a desperate limousine
        shout for fares.

        On the platform, fumbling for car keys
        I recall poets
        who fashion verse from train schedules.
        I wonder if this is

Low Italian

      the "more than we had"
      my grandfather had in mind
      for future generations.

I decide if Mussolini were here
he would make the trains run late.

George Guida

Sinatra
Drive,

> "...the extension of Frank Sinatra Drive will both benefit
> our communities and improve our environment..."
> —Bob Menendez, U. S. Congressman from New Jersey

no nearer home
    than a Hoboken train I ride,

        Sinatra Drive,

    da-bee-doo-da-day,

Sinatra Drive, I follow
    signs to explain the time
        between Oh, Sweet Romance yesterday and
    Where Have You gone? tomorrow.

Before refreshed by summer wind
from ignorance I ignored
directions, tips, that witchcraft of the Hudson.

    Oh, that crazy devil drive
    by the burnt out warehouse pilings,
        that walk along the skyline
      solo to the moon,
    blisters my dancin' feet.

Voice of another age,
    Let Someone Start Believin' in You,
      catches me as I cross
the Elysian baseball diamond croon,
      that first, that catchy melody
        of memory more
          than Remember How it Used to Feel?
to the old men in Hoboken Park, talking
      Frank and his romantic days
        before the movies

Low Italian

    before he was Frank, before
              the standards,
when he took love and got it
              under their skin.

   They wish now they could hollow out old bones,
      reinvent the marrow
    for tomorrows of yesterday.

      Toothless, huddled for the warmth
     of children playing, swinging,
  oh, swingin' strangers in the halflight,
eyes peering from worn windbreakers,
      friends of Sinatra, Frank's pals.

One of them walking First Street to his car,
   to deep America (for Hoboken never was),
     to his son, to his daughter, to the little ones,
    to the telling of memory,
   to Sinatra Drive,
    like Frank, cocks his finger, points it all around
     looks me to a stop and says,
  "They lock the doors
  and leave the windows open."

  And the voice sings to us again
      on our way to work
         from empty rooms,
   You'll Never Walk Alone, but
   that could be another song,
    not Frank's,
    not meant for us,
and we want so much,
just one more time to hear him sing
       just for us

Why doesn't he come back?

  A final asphalt path we follow
to waist-high barricades
   across the mouth of Sinatra Drive,

GEORGE GUIDA

kept by those who pose those questions

    Frank didn't compose
but knew to make his own.

Low Italian

Tina Scandul

A fool for your scandal, subrosa Italian,
How do I love you, Tina Scandul?

Your name the essence of *la differenza,*
free of a final vowel, free
as a walk across the mountains
from a long-lost *piazza.*

Scandul of the third generation,
apostrophe lost, but still Calabrese,
come to me in the evening
at our dialect revival.

The delicate dialect of your name
begins with an end stop, begins
with omission that makes me laugh, because
it makes me weep for years of Anns and Judys.

Yours is not the Scandul of denial,
but the genuine ring that weds us
in loss and recovery. A Scandul
covers up nothing and all.

I never thought to fall
for *una bella ragazza meridionale,*
or should I say, *'nu buon' raga'*?
But, oh, the sound of Scandul.

Over wine, pronounce us *un brindisi,*
Tina and me.
Here is a poem
for our wedding to be.

I will reach across time
to caress your lost o,
apocope reviving
mother, *patria, amore.*

In its place pin a tiny white bloom,
oh, girl of linguistic misrule.
The only word that means home
in this tongue always strange
is lovely, lovely Scandul.

Low Italian

A Fondness for Absent Flowers

They hoist the *giglio,* bear it
across Brooklyn and the sea
to a Sunday country dance
and a festival of blossoms in *bambini* tresses.

They find there *contadini*
they remember as uncles and aunts,
strangely young and hungry
for gestures to beauty and truth.

Drawn by wages to familiar, awful land,
dawn and dusk
they passed masters' gardens
strangling hill towns like beautiful snakes.

Starved by fences, like goats
they devoured rare petals
with voracious eyes long resigned
to vistas of clay and stone.

Was it enough to beg?
"*Signore,* today is Our Lady's day.
We pray only early blossoms
for *nostri figli* who never know them."

This is something.
A prayer for absent flowers,
for children's fondness for
beauty apart from death.

Bereft of lilies, of roses,
confined to hovels,
the stench of beasts defining them,
they left a landless land, recalling.

And from masters' malarial fields
new world *gigli* have sprung,
true enough to share,
too false to die in children's hair.

GLADIATOR'S LABYRINTH

Synthesized sambas salute me
in Italian B movies.

As I trundle, well-greaved, closer to death,
the sound inspires where it used to depress.

My mind drifts to an over-the-shoulder shot:

> INTERIOR — Two-door sedan by day.
> The camera catches flashing through the window
> the frosted face of a dead king.

A scene I must have watched in suicidal youth,
supine on an early couch,
afraid the time would never come
to see my love.

And now as the crowd cheers me on,
as I have tested the limits of fate,
I will pluck a gray hair from my chin,
and cleave it on my sword.

This gesture signifies nothing.

> In a recent epic film,
> Ancient Rome comes to life
> on wings of megabytes.

> Facades of facades flash across the screen
> through cascades of confetti,
> that Italian confection Italians shower
> upon me now,
> as I return triumphant
> to the place of my birth,
> the place whose name I have long forgotten
> how to speak — Rome and not Rome.

When I was a child
Italian soundtracks brought me down.

LOW ITALIAN

WHEN YOUR FAVORITE POET DIES

    he's usually ground under the wheels of a machine
    in the Italian sense of *macchina*,
        a vehicle someone drove over him
            for fun,
                in a hurry to get a lover off.

    Your favorite poet's heart
pumped blood that tinged his fingers pink,
pumped red blood to a thorax crushed
        by reckless youth
    in love with dune buggies,
    or street *scunizz'* in love
    with Alfa Romeos
borrowed from your wrecked bard's dream life.

    The News,
the names and their blood,
    lead you to imagine
you will have the good fortune to die,
        eyes surprised open
        and a permanent grin.

But have you suffered enough
        to suffer this way?
Have you abided
        museum, film, publication, award,
        possession by your generation's voice?
Have you discovered
an ironically simple hobby,
        like soccer or pederasty?
    At neither of which
    you were very much good.

George Guida

Poets are good
        at forgetting,

burying the dead with metaphor,
    Dantean twists of stiletto tongues.

They guess wistful maiden paths past
    saline rivers, the metonymy of which
            they forget.

They gliss pentatonic from minor,
    penning clefs to inflect registers
            only the tragic hear,

to trade toneless orgies gone berserk
    for circuses of salient phonemes,
    the pith of which
            they are good at forgetting.

Poets are good at....
    good at...
        forgetting,

like turns of centuries,
    like Augustine,
        like September from June.

Forgotten, forgiven, forgone,
    they are good.

They are good,
    like homemade wine, vinegar.

They are good,
    like echo.

They are good,
    like children.

Low Italian

Poets are good at forgetting,
    since they are hearts glued together
    and parlous,
        and they have to be.

Italian New Year

Tutta la roba si butta dalla finestra.
Everything goes out the window,
the Venetian shopkeeper warned,
 Get inside.

 Renewal

 Everything out the window
  Tutta la roba
 Couch, chair, chiffarobe

 But an Italian does not.

 My mother, my model Italian,
 fifty crates of Christmas in her cellar,
  closets full of broken Easter,
 clouds of Brooklyn memory above the table,
  raining olive oil on macaroni,

  oyster to rock,
  she clings to past,
 has my *sfatto* father recondition
 vinyl hassock, spaceship lamp.
 Nineteen-Sixty Spiegel Catalog

  Chino and angora snapshot
  Caputo's Candy Store
 Ten friends to steady the camera

  Impossible to think
  one New Year's Eve
 aboard the wearied sectional
  this woman of decades,
 of an Italian colony's mind,
 will want, like a promised recipe,
  everything out the window:

  Suddenly her husband rises
  to huddle nephew teams

Low Italian

who lift twin recliners,
drag them to the threshold.

11:59

ten-nine-eight-seven-six

Half-way gone
by the time Mama yells,
I can't do it.
These chairs are from Aunt Lena.

How smash Medici tombs?
How hurl relics of Pompeii
down Vesuvian maw?

Renewal

One New Year's Eve we spent in Venice
in a Chinese bistro:
Swiss tourists
Cover from the rain of memory
Someone else's table
While clocks chimed a new year of eternity,
we watched above.

GEORGE GUIDA

MY MOTHER MOVES TO VERMONT,

leaves my father and relatives
to "go frig themselves,"
packs her garden donkey, *presepe,* and venus fountain,
stocks up at the salumeria before she leaves,
figures up there they have those cows,
she'll buy the latticini local,
on the way up tastes Ben and Jerry's Vanilla Biscotti,
thinking she knows food,
decides to open her own ice cream parlor,
flavors she calls "different."
On a crisp fall morning
under her new apple tree she plans

The Menu:
chicken *parmigian'* chunk
cabuzell' surprise
pesto chocolate treat
sauce
scungill' ambrosia
macaroni and cream with the clams
sausage and peppers delight
fried *calamad'* crunch
steak *pizzaiol'* shake
smoked *mozzarell'* cheesecake
annisette, figs, and *pastaciott'*
    O.K.

Then, in the quiet of her Yankee yard,
her Italian stone porch,
she considers the wrought iron railing and beyond it,
clapboard houses, steeples, sugar maples,
and thinks she'll have to add another page:
What Americans Like.

Low Italian

My Mother's Ink

She got the first of it
the day my sister told her
she'd gotten engaged:
tattooed on the edge of her palm,
the tight face of Great Aunt Geremia,
so when she bit her hand
in Italian anger,
it scolded us for letting her be
the last to know.
As back-up,
on her thick upper arm
she had engraved
a double exposure of her long-dead mother,
a frown and a smile,
the kiss and the slap.

A day later when she met
the groom's dysfunctional American family
she got more,
the Italian flag, draped
from sturdy shoulders to ample bosom.

When she found out
the wedding wouldn't be in church,
of course she let a giant crucifix,
Christ, stigmata and all,
be scored into her back.
This one she would save
for the reception.

GEORGE GUIDA

TRADITIONS

My family has two:
cooking and construction.
In late years they've combined them.

My grandfather's designed a drill bit
fit to stir a pot of meat sauce
without mangling the *braciol'*.

My grandmother's working on a dough
that when left to bake in the sun
will hold bricks in place and taste
like the crust of a *pastaciott'*.

My uncles Peter and Dominick recently invented
a *gnocchi*-making attachment
for their hydraulic air compressor.

My great aunt Florence, all by herself,
has turned an ordinary *scuolapast'* into
a tool for sanding worn wood floors.

My mother and father have conspired
to reunite the family
by obliging us to sell these wares
at the retail outlet that used to be
their lonesome suburban home.

Low Italian

Your Cousin Dominick,

the quarter-ton guy in velour
you love like a part of your body,
the guy with the laugh like a bass hog squeal,
the guy who blurts through chortle,
"All right? All right? That's my best joke today!"
in a diner crammed with tourists
at whom, one by one, he stares too long.

Dominick took you for ziti,
to a place near the Madonna shrine
you never thought about before
your higher education,
when women and books were still a mystery;
Dominick, with the red comb-over
that wasn't called so then, just hair;
Dominick, who fed the dogs, no matter where,
no matter whose—your dog, my dog, the priest's dog,
the neighbor's dog, when she took off to Vegas—
always with table scraps and stories about work.

The diner tourists, now more part of you than he,
stare back at him with eyes that wither him in yours.
He still grows tomatoes, cucumbers, zucchini,
tending them the way you read for class.
Dominick still summarizes tabloids
on the stoop, on the dock
where he fishes with a bamboo pole
for stasis.

He is married to his mother,
her sauce and washer-dryer.

Dominick went on a diet
twenty years ago, five months long,
gained thirty pounds,
couldn't in the end deny himself
the pleasures you used to share.

JIMI HENDRIX INFLUENCES ITALIAN AMERICAN PARENTS FROM BROOKLYN

      Scene: A red house (over yonder) in suburbia.
      There are two American-made cars in the driveway.
      There are lawn ornaments. It is Sunday. A sauce is
      up. Everyone is home.

DAD: Let me ask you something, son
      Are you experienced?
      Well, I am...
      and let me tell ya,
      it's very nice.
      I remember
      when you were small,
      you could get your little mind together
      and crawl across the living room
      to the Christmas tree:
      not necessarily a real tree,
      but byooteeful.

MOM: The other day when I was sweeping
      you know, the crumbs
      off the kitchen floor,
      somebody drove up in front
      and started beeping
      and I couldn't do any more,
      so I came back in
      with the package from the UPS,
      and I had no cash,
      so I gave the guy a personal check.
      Your little sister was watching
      the idiot box,
      and your father was out on the deck,
      and then I heard him yell,
      "Mary!,
      bring out the annisette!"

Low Italian

Barney on Long Island

Barney the purple dinosaur
comes to an Italian child's party. He sings
"I love you, you love me,
we're a happy family,"
as all the aunts and uncles join in.

The father squeezes Barney's tail.
"What material do they fill this with?"
he wonders, while on his knee
Barney dandles a *mamadell'*,
not fully comprehending what that is.

The deck is rocking with music
and Barney's muffled guffaws,
when appears the mother
with a tray of eggplant rollatini.

Barney is sweating by now,
soaked almost through the fake fur,
when Nonna Julia pinches his insensate cheek.
He's been chasing chubby children
for an hour now. He's soon due
on someone else's deck,

when appears the mother
with a mountainous plate of ziti
and other gestures Italian.
Barney slowly shakes his heavy head.

"What, Barney? You're not gonna eat?"
the mother asks, already knowing the answer.
Barney stalks off, across the yard.
The mother follows.

She pulls him by the leathern paw
back to the mammoth umbrellaed table,
where sit a dozen relatives,
who think it's cute the way the children

smash his massive feet with garden rocks.

"Stay a while, Barney," the father insists,
goading for him to show
the human face beneath.

The mother pushes Barney down
before another plate, glass of wine, and *tazza*
still upside down, an evening of memory
and espresso to come.
Barney struggles to escape,
but the father claps his shoulder
and gives his head a yank.

An hour later, Barney finds himself
about to burst his costume,
part of the spectacle dating back
nearly to prehistoric times.

Low Italian

Down These Very Nice Streets
or
The Endless Conversation

(a poem for too many voices)

Capo: Maybe you don't believe me when I say this
 but back then everything was very nice.
 Don't get me wrong. Tough. But very nice.

 Son: I want to believe you, but history...

Capo: It was more fair then. It was like a big family.
 If you had a problem, we all had a problem.
 You left your doors open.
 Someone always wanted you to try new wine.

 Son: I like my privacy, and
  wine has always upset my stomach.

Capo: Ask anybody. Those were good days.
 None of the boys got into trouble.
 And the girls never cursed.

 Son: I have been imprisoned by these stories
  from before I could speak.

   Ma: Who wants more macaroni?
   Is your father done with his plate?
    Did you have enough?
    Who gets coffee?
    Milk?
    Sugar?
    Annisette?
    Canoli?

Capo: You can't find good canoli anymore.

 Company #1: No, now,

> you gotta look.

Company #2: Used to be good canoli
> on every corner.

Company #3: Now,
> you gotta look.

Son: I have been imprisoned by tales
> of good canoli.

Capo: You don't know what good food is.

Son: What have I been eating?

Ma: I'll save the meatballs
> for after dessert,
> in case you get hungry again.

Capo: We were never hungry.
Who ate better than us?
Tripe. Prosciut'. Cabuzzell'.
Delicious.

Company #2: Cabuzzell' is the, ah...

Capo: Goat's head. Delicious.

Son: Should I long for the head of a goat?

Ma: You can't find them in the supermarkets.

Son: Thank the Madonna
> in whom I no longer believe.

Company #3: Madonna mi!
> This coffee's hot.

Ma: You want it cold?
> What do you expect?

Son: I expect someday to know why cheesecake
must be wet.

Low Italian

Capo: At the restaurants out here they never have the real cheesecake.

Ma: Who cares?
I can make it better at home.

Capo: But you can't get the good mozzarell'.

Son: Oh, to taste of the good mozzarell'.

Ma: That's the secret to manicotts.

Capo: Your manicotts'll never be my mother's.

Company #1: Not bad, though.

Son: I never ate grandma's manicotts.
Who was she?

Ma: A real pain in the ass.

Capo: She did everything for us.

Ma: And she made me miserable.

Son: I am the offspring of misery.

Capo: You're just like my grandfather.
He loved manicotts.

Son: Ricotta too upsets my stomach

Company #3: The best.

Ma: None of you know what's good.

GEORGE GUIDA

GERMOCC' AND GEBUCC'

> "You're a *mucc*!"
> "What's a *mucc*?"
> "I don't know."
> —dialogue from Martin Scorsese's *Mean Streets*

I never thought I would have to say this
in, like, words, but
aaaayyyy, hey-heeeyyyy!

    Let's discuss the construction
    of my culturally bifurcated,
trifurcated self and the influence
of that identity formation on my conception of
gender roles in relation to dominant subject positions.

Blow me,
you son of a fag whore!

    It isn't yet clear the extent to which
    exploitation of the subaltern as a dilemma
    qua dilemma will continue to occupy our intellectuals
    of the first rank, but it appears certain, at least,
    that it will remain the focal point
    of the most meretricious commentary.

Go back to your fuckin' country!

    It's in this part of the poem, if that's what you want
to call it, that you want a referee
    or some other Italian or at least ethnic to step in.
stop the fight and tell you what the hell a *germocc'* is.

    C'mon! You know that.
    You know what that is.
    It's like...aaahh...aaaaayyyyy!

    Gebucc': Person of scant intellectual prowess,

Low Italian

prone to spells of idiotic behavior.

Same as a *germocc'*,
but a little different.

   We're getting locked in again.

Fly, oh treasured significance of *germocc'!*
Gebucc', be free!

   What'd I say? What'd I just say?

Alma Mater

I returned an Italian American,
        and no one knew me from the Ivy.

The guard at the gate
        threatened to revoke my overcoat.

Students finding themselves
   lost their reflections in my patent leather shoes.

I limped across campus with no organ to grind,
        so researchers lent me a monkey.

On the library façade Hegel and Marx
        bookended Boccaccio.

When I searched the catalog for Italian Americans.
        The screen asked, "Who wants to know?"

      This is how I discovered America uneasy
   being red white and green,
when the registrar struck my name from the record.

Low Italian

Aeneas

for Bob

I. Haven

Fill me, Madonna, with inky tears
for the man of gnocchi,
diabetic in epic appetite
for American cherry pie and candy.
Sing in me an aria
of grappa-soaked logomachies
with whisky senses.

I have shed tears,
these inky tears for you, my friend,
as you pleasure afternoons
of shapely artists who,
in homage to our mother,
beautiful land of olive groves, of sea,
of bygone dust on malarial corpses,
with chisel and sweat
limn our beauty.

You slide, a man in her arms, like a tear
down the cheek of America,
refinding, refining, redefining Rome,
Naples, Palermo, Pompeii,
geographer, historian, myth.

II. City

Your father's mask unmans you,
a shrink suggests,
as he lies broken and Italian
(for often they are synonyms)
in your mind, singing *"Ridi, Pagliaccio!"*
clinging to an old world
friable as ancient bones.

Himself, he died and journeyed.
What's left to accomplish?
Find her—called Italia.
Strap on a mail of names,
absorb her blows,
but wonder to yourself
who cares for Latin,
let alone its bastard kin?
If you carry the memory of your father
to business lunches, cafés, to rendezvous,
can you blame a woman?

    III. Strange Meetings

With your oxymoron, a strange family,
practice your ritual, gold's curse
on humanity: the divorce.
Wander, Great King, to the urban underworld
where ghostly figures join you
in rooms of gloaming, beg you
to beget a race
of bricklayers, policemen, secretaries,
who live in distant suburbs,
returning every second Sunday
to visit your invisible *città*.

Low Italian

Why Italians Will Save the World

The murals of Paestum's secret chambers
give us naked lads of Magna Graecia
prone together on rich rugs,
feeding one another tender grapes
plucked from seaside hill vines
down which hand in hand
or hand in hand with tribal girls
they gamboled like wild goats.

These Italic Greeks in touch with femininity
never could conquer Samnite hordes,
but built temples to subdue
native women who in surrender
became the mothers of ancient Rome.

Togas off of shoulders
held all Rome's power in light fall
to mosaic floors of victory's thrall to virtue.
When women fell from view,
so too Rome inclined
and in submission to pagan want
gifted Italians to a world awaiting
a folk to keep wars small.

They argued only how to elevate
comely mother to Godhead,
fought most fiercely battles
to bankroll a succession of Madonnas
gathering to their bosoms
the issue of Empire's unconquered tribes.

I'll Never Die Italian

I'll live always under English glass,
and each day pray to gods of marble
for a solid shelf, and each day
pull my wilted dandelions
from the cold ground, to inter them
by night, like thoughts exhume themselves,
to bloom the next time crystal.

I'll live in the flow of *mai*,
I mean never, and never mind chiaroscuro.
I'll live in constant pursuit
of my purse and suit, and sweetness and light
made flesh and the first letter
of the Roman alphabet.

I and this new world will not decline.
I will be always able to climb the tower
with its view of what's to come,
and leap to my life in a sea
that buoyed *antenati*,
I mean the one between here and Italy.

I'll outlive the vagabonds,
the children of Samnites, Normans, Goths
who call themselves my kin,
by shedding my skin and hair and accent,
and forgetting always *non dimenticare*.

When we got here, wasn't that
a song we used to sing?

Low Italian

Ci sentiamo

Nel passato, nel futuro
ci sentiamo,
quando mai più fai l'amante,
quando non più faccio l'amore
che zoppica, ubriac'.

Ci sentiamo, ti giuro, benchè
non ci vediamo più.

Noi non andiamo a spasso
sotto il ponte ponente
che finisce nel pozzo, nel buio
d'un'onda sparita facciante.

Ci compro cioccolata
troppo cara da mangiare,
ma sotto la luna
li tiriamo fuori,
ammiriamo ogni pezzo,
ogni barlume azzurro.

Noi non ci sposiamo
poiché siamo già legati,
anche se non ci si rendiamo
conto dei nostri tesori.

Guardami, Guardami,
perché ci falliamo,
ci faliscono gli occhi,
e non ci asteniamo.

Ci sentiamo quando
beviamo al volere di
confessare quest'amore,
i giorni che noi potremmo darci
nel giardino di zucchini
circondato dai cani nostri
che non saprèbbero
neanche i suoi nomi.

Ci sentiamo sempre,
ci sentiamo, parlando
passando,
volendo,
morendo,
ci sentiamo spesso,
ma non ci conosciamo
mai più.

Low Italian

LA VITA SAREBBE BELLA ANCHE SE

    tu
          con bocca
            di rifiuti macinati
mi disprezzassi e sprizzassi.

        In qualche luogo cresce l'erbe.
        Da qualche parte ondeggia il mare.

      La vita sarebbe bella anche se

    tu   con occhi selvaggi

mi odiassi come costumi odierni.
        Dappertutto le colline ci sorridono.
        La briza ride ai nostri peccatti.

      La vita sarebbe bella anche se

    tu   con puzz'a naso

mi sconfessassi come prete sconcio,

        sarebbe anche bella se

      di notte una farfalla
     di notte sola congiurasse la conquista
di nostro mondo dal ribelle vertice d'alberello
e poi, come uccello, si spegnesse
        dove non guarda nessuno.

Life Would Be Fine Even If

you
                      with a mouthful of chewed trash

scorned and sprinkled me.
                  Someplace grass grows.
              Somewhere the sea laps the shore.

        Life would be fine even if

you   with savage eyes

despised me like modern morals.
                Everywhere the hills smile upon us.
                The breeze laughs at our sins.

        Life would be fine even if

you   with nose in the air

renounced me like an indecent priest,

        would even be fine if

        by night a lone moth
     nightly plotted conquest of our world
  from a rebellious shrubtop
and then, like a bird, died
              where no one watches.

Low Italian

Repeat After Me

        I am not a dago.
        I am not a dago.
        I am not a dago.
    I am not a dago.

      I am not.
      I am not.
      I am not.
I am not a word from before the war.
I am not a Nebraskan's idea of pizza.
I am not.

I will not be.
    I will not.
    I will not.
I will not gesticulate.
I will not screw up my face.

      I should not do these things.
I should not well up at memories.
I should not muse over pasts and futures as I walk.
I should not kiss cheeks.
I should not kiss my rosary, not knowing why.
I should not lie in the sun without guilt.
I should not allow love to distract me from work.
I should not recriminate the charges of feeling against me.
I should not get carried away.

    I might not.
    I might not.
I might not see the patria again.

I should not call it patria.

I might not live to see tomorrow.
I might not be sad in this exuberant land.
I might not call myself Italian.
I might not understand what I am saying.

I might.

But then I might not.

But then I will not.
    I will not.
    I will not.
        I will not attempt to explain.
        I will never write it down.

Low Italian

Personal References

Almost all of them Italian.

    For variety's sake

        I want to list a Scot.

"May we contact your references?"
                              an employer asks.

Certainly,
    if they're not out admiring Baroque facades,
    if they're not out taking espresso,
        chocolate-dipped biscotti,
            at sidewalk cafés,

    if they're not out strolling, whistling,
        hands behind their backs
            as they stare at dappled rivers,
    if they're not out stalking lovers' apartments,
        like disrobed monarchs,

    if their minds and hearts aren't so engaged,

        they may tell you who I am.

Zen Italian

"La vita è bella. So'
fatto così," quoth
the zen
Italian.

"It's all the same to me,"
he says,
with his shoulder shrug
and café cup.
"Go see
what you wanna see."

"Nessun' dorma"'s his
favorite song:
The universe
in every verse
should know his mind,
should hear his voice.

"In vino veritas,"
he lies and gulps
a glass of bathtub red.
Un brindisi:
"That everything we think
we know is just
spettacolo."

From his mother
he knows
the highest truth of all:
that one can live
with everyone
and never understand
a soul.

Low Italian

An Italian Friend

An Italian friend calls to say,

I read your book.
You are a great writer.
I didn't understand a word.

VIA Folios
A refereed book series dedicated to Italian studies and the culture of Italian Americans in North America.

EMANUEL CARNEVALI
Furnished Rooms
Vol. 43, forthcoming

ANTHONY ELLIS, ET AL.
Shifting Borders Negotiating Places
Vol. 42, Interdisciplinary Studies, $18.00

GEORGE GUIDA
Low Italian
Vol. 41, Poetry, forthcoming

FRED GARDAPHÈ, PAOLO GIORDANO, ANTHONY JULIAN TAMBURRI
Introducing Italian Americana: Generalities on Literature and Film
Vol. 40, Italian American Studies, $10.00

DANIELA GIOSEFFI
Blood Autumn/Autunno di sangue
Vol. 39, Poetry, $15.00

FRED MISURELLA
Lies to Live by
Vol. 38, Stories, $15.00

STEVEN BELLUSCIO
Constructing a Bibliography
Vol. 37

ANTHONY JULIAN TAMBURRI, ED.
Italian Cultural Studies 2002
Vol. 36, Essays, $18.00

BEA TUSIANI
con amore
Vol. 35, Memoir, $19.00

FLAVIA BRIZIO-SKOV, ED.
Reconstructing Societies in the Aftermath of War
Vol. 34, History/Cultural Stud., $30.00

A.J. TAMBURRI, M.S. RUTHENBERG, G. PARATI, AND B. LAWTON, EDS.
Italian Cultural Studies 2001
Vol. 33, Essays, $18.00

ELIZABETH GIOVANNA MESSINA, ED.
In Our Own Voices
Vol. 32, Ital. Amer. Studies, $25.00

STANISLAO G. PUGLIESE
Desperate Inscriptions
Vol. 31, History, $12.00

ANNA CAMAITI HOSTERT & ANTHONY JULIAN TAMBURRI, EDS.
Screening Ethnicity
Vol. 30, Ital. Amer. Culture, $25.00

G. PARATI & B. LAWTON, EDS.
Italian Cultural Studies
Vol. 29, Essays, $18.00

HELEN BAROLINI
More Italian Hours & Other Stories
Vol. 28, Fiction, $16.00

FRANCO NASI, A CURA DI
Intorno alla Via Emilia
Vol. 27, Culture, $16.00

ARTHUR L. CLEMENTS
The Book of Madness and Love
Vol. 26, Poetry, $10.00

JOHN CASEY, ET. AL
Imagining Humanity
Immagini dell'umanità
Vol. 25, Interdisciplinary Studies, $18.00

ROBERT LIMA
Sardinia • Sardegna
Vol. 24, Poetry, $10.00

DANIELA GIOSEFFI
Going On
Vol. 23, Poetry, $10.00

ROSS TALARICO
The Journey Home
Vol. 22, Poetry, $12.00

EMANUEL DI PASQUALE
The Silver Lake Love Poems
Vol. 21, Poetry, $7.00

JOSEPH TUSIANI
Ethnicity
Vol. 20, Selected Poetry, $12.00

JENNIFER LAGIER
Second Class Citizen
Vol. 19, Poetry, $8.00

FELIX STEFANILE
The Country of Absence
Vol. 18, Poetry, $9.00

PHILIP CANNISTRARO
Blackshirts
Vol. 17, History, $12.00

LUIGI RUSTICHELLI, ED.
Seminario sul racconto
Vol. 16, Narrativa, $10.00

LEWIS TURCO
Shaking the Family Tree
Vol. 15, Poetry, $9.00

LUIGI RUSTICHELLI, ED.
Seminario sulla drammaturgia
Vol. 14, Theater/Essays, $10.00

Fred L. Gardaphè
Moustache Pete is Dead!
Long Live Moustache Pete!
Vol. 13, Oral literature, $10.00

JONE GAILLARD CORSI
Il libretto d'autore, 1860–1930
Vol. 12, Criticism, $17.00

HELEN BAROLINI
Chiaroscuro: Essays of Identity
Vol. 11, Essays, $15.00

T. PICARAZZI AND W. FEINSTEIN, EDS.
An African Harlequin in Milan
Vol. 10, Theater/Essays, $15.00

JOSEPH RICAPITO
Florentine Streets and Other Poems
Vol. 9, Poetry, $9.00

FRED MISURELLA
Short Time
Vol. 8, Novella, $7.00

NED CONDINI
Quartettsatz
Vol. 7, Poetry, $7.00

ANTHONY JULIAN TAMBURRI, ED.
MARY JO BONA, INTROD.
Fuori: Essays by Italian/American Lesbians and Gays
Vol. 6, Essays, $10.00

ANTONIO GRAMSCI
PASQUALE VERDICCHIO,
TRANS. & INTROD.
The Southern Question
Vol. 5, Social Criticism, $5.00

DANIELA GIOSEFFI
Word Wounds and Water Flowers
Vol. 4, Poetry, $8.00

WILEY FEINSTEIN
Humility's Deceit: Calvino Reading Ariosto Reading Calvino
Vol. 3, Criticism, $10.00

PAOLO A. GIORDANO, ED.
Joseph Tusiani: Poet, Translator, Humanist
Vol. 2, Criticism, $25.00

ROBERT VISCUSI
Oration Upon the Most Recent Death of Christopher Columbus
Vol. 1, Poetry, $3.00

Published by BORDIGHERA, INC., an independently owned not-for-profit scholarly organization that has no legal affiliation to the University of Central Florida, The John D. Calandra Italian American Institute, or State University of New York—Stony Brook.